IMAGES
of England

WANTAGE

Statue of King Alfred the Great, c. 1876. King Alfred, the West Saxon King was born at Wantage, A.D.849. This statue was commissioned by Colonel Robert Loyd-Lindsay VC (who became Lord Wantage), for which he paid 2000 guineas. The sculptor, Prince Victor Ferdinand Franz Eugen Gustaf Constantin Friedrich of Hohenlohe-Langenburg, (a title he renounced and became Count Gleichen) was a nephew of Queen Victoria. The Queen allowed him to build a studio in the grounds of St James' Palace where this early photograph was probably taken.

IMAGES
of England

WANTAGE

Compiled by
Irene Hancock

TEMPUS

First published 1995, reprinted 1999
Copyright © Irene Hancock, 1995

Tempus Publishing Limited
The Mill, Brimscombe Port,
Stroud, Gloucestershire, GL5 2QG

ISBN 0 7524 0146 7

Typesetting and origination by
Tempus Publishing Limited
Printed in Great Britain by
Midway Clark Printing, Wiltshire

Contents

The Town Hall, c. 1910. This Town Hall was opened in 1878 and sold by the Urban District Council in 1954, for £5,400 with subsequent loss to the community. Orchard House was bought as a replacement to be used as Council Offices.

Introduction

Wantage was spelt in the past in a variety of ways - Wanetinze, Wanating, Wantinge. The town developed from an ancient market town nestling in the Vale of the White Horse with the Portway passing through it and the Ridgeway high above.

The early settlement was important for the Saxons and their court, which travelled the Kingdom and was in residence in Wantage when Alfred the Great was born in 849, as recorded by his biographer, Asser. The precise location of this event has not been determined and probably any evidence of their habitation has not withstood weather, time and the Danes. Alfred left the town in his will to his wife Alswythe. In 997 Ethelred held a wintenagemot (witan) in Wantage to draw up a Code of Laws for the administration of justice.

The settlement's position on the spring line encouraged early habitation. The presence of productive arable land, meadowland and pastures for sheep contributed to the suitability of the land for agriculture. The Letcombe Brook, that runs through, Wantage was later to provide water for corn mills, for the washing and fulling of wool and the tanning of hides and skins.

The Domesday survey states that, 'the King held Wantage in demesne' and it was worth £61. It remained in Royal hands for 400 years but was alienated from the Crown by Richard I when it passed to the Earl of Albemarle, and then the Earl of Pembroke by marriage. On the marriage of the Earl's daughter, Matilda, the Manor was given to Fulk Fitzwaryn, a descendant of Guarine de Meez who arrived during the Norman conquest. His son Sir Ivo Fitzwaryn was the father of Alice who became the wife of Richard (Dick) Whittington, thrice Lord Mayor of London.

During the Civil War Royalists and Roundheads were often quartered in the area. Twice Charles I stayed with Sir George Wilmot of Charlton on his way to Oxford. The roundheads could have been responsible for the destruction of the Market Cross erected by the Earl of Bath.

With the focus of a wide square green the mediaeval market town of 1000 inhabitants thrived, with Town, Priorshold and Wanting Brian Manors and the production of corn, butter, wool, hides and animals for market. Large houses were built, at Belmont, Wanting Brian, The Ham and at Charlton.

Charities and trusts were set up in the fifteenth century for the poor and needy. To discourage misappropriation of funds an Act of Parliament was passed in 1597 ordering the setting up a body of twelve inhabitants to form the Governors of Town Lands and to legally deal with the charity funds.

Transport to and from Wantage has never been easy. From the early days of the stage coaches, leaving a few times a week to London, to the public transport of the twentieth century, but Wantage's relative isolation has meant that the beautiful countryside around the town has been retained.

The Wantage arm of the Wilts & Berks Canal was cut in the early nineteenth century, giving people easier access to the area. The town became known, for a while, as 'Black Wantage' as drunkenness and crime increased, disadvantages that somewhat offset the advantages of the increased trade.

Mr William Ormond and influential citizens, anxious about the future of the town, initiated the passing of an Act of Parliament in 1828 for 'lighting, watching, paving, cleansing and improving the town'. Commissioners were appointed for the execution of the Act. The Victorians contributed extensively to the town. The appointment of a young Vicar, the Revd William Butler made an impact; in addition to spiritual guidance he promoted education and improved social conditions for working people. His pride and joy was the founding of the Community of St Mary the Virgin on Camel Hill. The Baptists had survived religious persecution and their present chapel was built in Mill Street. The Wesleyan community erected a chapel in Newbury Street. Colonel Robert and the Hon Harriet Loyd-Lindsay took up residence in Lockinge in a house presented to them by Harriet's father, Lord Overstone. Their close presence was to have a pronounced influence on the development of Wantage.

With the coming of the Great Western Railway and a station locally at Challow in 1860 and later at Wantage Road, the canal was doomed. Initially, though, the inaccessibility of the station was a problem for townspeople but this was solved by the construction of a special tramway linking the town with the station. During the Second World War American servicemen were stationed at Grove Airfield and their transport churned up so much mud on the road that the trams were unable to run. The growth of transport by road finally sealed the fate of the tramway.

The Charlton House Estate was bought in 1947 by the Ministry of Supply to house employees of the Atomic Energy Research Establishment and about 400 houses were built. Further sales of agricultural land for housing followed and Wantage has seen much development and population growth in postwar years.

At the end of the nineteenth century the Commissioners were replaced by the Urban District Council. In 1974 the County boundaries were realigned and Wantage was assimilated into Oxfordshire to be administered by the Vale of White Horse District Council, with a Town Council having greatly reduced power.

One
The Market Place

Wantage from the air, c. 1925. An open Market Place, a lone statue and few people. Sun blinds are shielding the north side, and Wallingford Street is clearly seen. The town is surrounded by fields and trees, houses, and shops with gardens. The parish church is in the bottom right-hand corner. The tramway terminus is visible off Mill Street. Stirling's field can be seen in the top left-hand corner and, below, haystacks on a farm.

The Market Place, c. 1854. The railings enclose the town pond. In 1861 the Commissioners ordered that the pond be puddled with clay from top to bottom. The buildings on the South side have hardly changed, the 'old' Town Hall built in 1835 was demolished to make space for the King Alfred Statue. Thomas Wilkins' waggon departed for London from the Crown of Old England on the right. James Thatcher's house was demolished in the late nineteenth century. This north side was redeveloped during the 1960s and 70s.

The Market Place, c. 1854. Charles Saunders' shop is on the left, selling china, glass and earthenware. He was also the Registrar for births, marriages and deaths. There was a printing office, and on the immediate right a chemist, a general grocer, and Rose & Hatton was a linen and woollen drapers. Before this Town Hall was built an earlier Market House existed, really a superior type of shed, raised on posts. Beneath was a lock-up, into which prisoners were lowered through a trap door. Children were said to taunt prisoners through a grill.

The 'Old' Town Hall, c. 1860. This is a rear view of the Hall showing the closeness to the present Green & Co building on the left. On the right is now Barclay's Bank and Badger's men's outfitting store. Designed as a Town Hall it was built in 1835 with public subscription; the open space below was used as a Market Hall and included a savings bank and lock-up. The people of Wantage considered it an ugly building - the architect was better known as a specialist in the designing of workhouses.

The 'new' Town Hall, c. 1878. When Colonel Loyd-Lindsay offered to give a statue of King Alfred to the town, the centre of the Market Place was selected as the most suitable site, so the old Town Hall had to go! Townspeople were happy to agree to this hall being demolished and Colonel Loyd-Lindsay, therefore, purchased the Falcon Inn on the corner of Grove Street (for £900) to provide a site for a new one. The cost of erecting the Hall was met by subscription: Colonel Loyd-Lindsay and his father-in-Law, Lord Overstone, gave £1,400, the town and neighbourhood £925, the County contributed £700, to hold the Court in the building, and sale of materials from the 'old' Town Hall raised £265. The architect was Mr Tasker of London and Colonel Loyd-Lindsay's agent, Mr Dolby, supervised the building. The bricks were made near Beedon, Newbury and the timber prepared at Ardington. The opening ceremony took the form of a lunch presided over by Mr H Denis de Vitre, when after lengthy speeches, Colonel Loyd-Lindsay handed to Mr de Vitre the key of the new hall. The building, on the right, a shoe warehouse and the former Globe Inn were also purchased by Colonel Loyd-Lindsay and became Mrs Sansum's shoe warehouse, a register office for servants and a coffee tavern. The Coffee House Company was formed in 1880.

The Market Place and Statue, c. 1909. Two years after the unveiling of the King Alfred statue the Commissioners wished to affix a descriptive plaque. The suggestion was taken up with alacrity by Colonel Loyd-Lindsay who provided the words to be displayed. The plaque was originally mounted in a sloping position and children used it as a slide. The lettering became worn and so brass nails were hammered in to make this pastime uncomfortable.

King Alfred Statue, c. 1905. With the exception of the Post Office Vaults (saved from demolition, primarily, by John Betjeman), the buildings in the background have vanished. On the right Mr Liddiard's shop became Mr Gibbs' printing premises and then, in the 1930s, the new Regent Cinema. Next door, an impressive building, a bank for years, was demolished in favour of a more 'functional' building.

13

King Alfred Statue, c. 1920. The plaque was moved to preserve the lettering, the metal was reburnished, recut and secured vertically on the base. The trough, here serving its original purpose was moved to the Recreation Ground but later returned by the Town Council to be used as a flower holder. The drinking fountain was presented by Miss Maria Houblon, sister of the Revd Archer Houblon, appointed Vicar of Wantage in 1880.

Bird's eye view, c. 1930. A view from the parish church tower with cars now taking over in the Market Place. In the distance, is St Katharine's tower. On the left is the new white house, Thermidor, built by Mr Henry Thurston, Managing Director of the Foundry. Nearby Stirlings, is the home of the Hon Beatrice Goschen built by William Stirling who purchased the Manor of Wantage Brian in 1752. The varied and interesting roof line of the north side dominates this view in the bright sunshine.

Market Place, c. 1939. There is an increase in the number of cars parked in 'The Square', otherwise little has changed, but the Regent Cinema, built in the 1930s and much disliked by Sir John Betjeman, has now appeared. He hoped that, 'no more buildings as jazzily discordant as the cinema would be allowed to insult Wantage's old streets.'

King Alfred's Statue, c. 1946. The wheel arch on the car in the background is painted white, a requirement in the war years to enable it to be seen during the blackouts of the 1940s. The statue has suffered in the War, the axe blade is missing, reputedly removed by Americans stationed at Grove Airfield and allegedly taken to the D Day landings. AA motor cycles and sidecars like this one will be remembered by many; cars displaying an AA badge would always receive a salute from the AA patrol man.

15

The Victoria Cross Gallery, c. 1920. The Bear, Barclay's Bank and Arbery's shop are in local red brick with varied patterns between the windows. Accommodation in the VC Gallery was provided for the Fire Brigade in 1910. Previously the fire engine had been kept in the parish church, in the 'old' Town Hall and in Portway. At the beginning of the nineteenth century this building was the Red Lion Inn, but it was sold to the Corn Exchange Company and the courtyard at the rear roofed over in 1865. Subsequently the Wantage Commissioners bought the Corn Exchange buildings, the dwelling house, including fittings, desks, chairs, clock, etc., in 1893 for £1,850. It was renamed the VC Gallery in November 1900, on the day Lord Wantage gave the Desanges' Victoria Cross paintings to Wantage. The bricks placed in an oblong in the Market Place were often referred to as the 'pig pavement', and indicate where the hurdles would be set up for animals on market days.

'The Black Bear' and Victoria Cross Gallery, 1904. An early photograph of the wooden bear, thought to be black. The embossed lion remains as a reminder of the Red Lion Inn. On the back of this postcard is written, 'the grapes are said to have been taken down and carried through two wars by local men.' Men of the Berkshire Yeomanry once attempted to paint the black bear white, but the escapade ended tragically. The forecourt became covered in white paint, the bear was broken and the yeomen bruised!.

The Bear Hotel, c. 1920. Another 'bear', this one could be brown, holding the grapes in the other side of the mouth. Barclays Bank have moved into the part of the building vacated by Belcher's cycle shop. The Ormond's house is just visible between the two buildings.

The Bear Hotel, c. 1930. The Bear Hotel is older than its facade suggests. Tradesmen's tokens were issued by Thomas Hurdman of the Bear in the seventeenth century, each embossed with a bear and chain. In 1957 the brown wooden bear was replaced with a new one at a cost of approximately £100. The brown bear which had given good service was painted white and placed in the courtyard but was stolen in the following year, including its grapes which were said to have been made for the original bear.

The Bear Hotel Courtyard, c. 1912. A beautiful cobbled courtyard with, under the archway, steps and a dark wooden bannister rail leading up to the coffee room. Mr Charles Mayo was ostler here for 46 years. He died in 1910 and two foxhound puppies from the hotel followed his funeral procession. His son, William Mayo succeeded him as groom and gardener.

The Victoria Cross Gallery, c. 1900. The VC Gallery housed forty six paintings, mostly of men, soldiers, sailors and civilians, who were the first recipients of the Victoria Cross, by the artist Louis William Desanges. The paintings had been exhibited at the Crystal Palace and Lord Wantage bought the collection fearing it would be dispersed. They were presented to the town of Wantage and placed in the care and management of the Urban District Council. The painting of Lord Wantage, now in the Civic Hall, is on the right.

Victoria Cross Painting No 19, c. 1904. The VC paintings were photographed by Gale & Polden Ltd and issued as postcards. This painting illustrates Surgeon Mouat and Sergeant Major Wooden, treating the wounds of Colonel Morris after the charge of the Light Brigade at Balaklava on 25 October 1854. In 1952 the paintings were distributed on permanent loan to military authorities by the Urban District Council. Painting No 19 is in the Officers' Mess of the Queen's Royal Lancers in Osnabrück, Germany.

Kent & Son, c. 1930. An interesting photograph and an effective advertisement, worth inclusion in this collection for the lamps alone. Self-drive vehicles were also available. There is only one petrol pump, dispensing Pratts Ethyl Petrol. They also sold Hall's sanitary washable distemper.

Kent & Son and King Alfred's Head, c. 1911. Kent & Son, was one of the older businesses of Wantage. Cycles and spares were sold at Kent's ironmongers and accommodation for cyclists provided at the King Alfred's Head. They also offered stabling, loose boxes and posting. Carriers left the King Alfred's Head on prescribed days for the villages. The pinnacle was removed during this century.

Kent & Son, c. 1938. Kent's always exhibited a good selection of items for sale outside, even up to the 1960s. The Red & White Cafe on the left was followed by Farmer's the hairdresser and tobacconist and next door was a baker.

Corner of the Market Place, c. 1910. A Chapman & Son photograph. The lamp informs us that Lewis Penney is now the owner of the draper's shop on the left and above the window, we can see was that it was lately owned by Bromley. A J Belcher is selling cycles, next door, and then there is James Lovegrove, tailor (now Badger's Menswear). The Alfred Grocery Store, sold groceries for at least half a century and is now Geoffrey Bailey Shoes.

The Market Place, c. 1904. We are now moving to the right, around the Market Place - these shops were refronted in the previous century. Edward J Blood is the jeweller and clock maker, the clock and windows are bordered artistically with cream bricks. Francis Pegler has a large building for selling carpets and linoleum. Cycles are sold from a house converted into a shop on the corner of Mill Street and Grove Street. The horse and waggon is advertising Rock Well Brewery from Wallingford Street. George Wigmore was a saddler and harness maker.

The North West Corner, c. 1900. An earlier photograph of this picturesque corner. The Bell Inn looks the same today. The Baptist Church is very white and new and the building next door has a stable entrance. Hughes, the bootmaker, has moved from Mill Street. The blinds were held up with posts. The Commissioners reprimanded shopkeepers for letting blinds drop too low, restricting access for pedestrians walking on the pavements. The clock on the Town Hall was presented to the town by Mr E Ormond.

The North Side, c. 1939. Continuing changes have replaced the saddler's shop with Walter Liddiard, selling His Master's Voice radios. Arthur and Edith Harris were confectioners. The tea rooms were upstairs and tea dances were held. A ground floor could also be booked for children's parties. There is good view of Ernest and Frederick Cottrell's butcher's shop. William Palmer, next door, was also a butcher.

The Market Place, 'facing East', c. 1930. The Cottrells were in business in the Market Place for more than a century, but not always in this shop. They owned two farms, the King's a 200 acres estate, with cattle, sheep and pigs and Grove Hams, 50 acres, where calves were fattened. The fish shop was on the other side of the Market Place. Mr W H Palmer, was the owner of a long established business specialising in English meat and advertising modern refrigeration, in the 1930s.

Tom Reveley, c. 1899. Tom Reveley became well-known as a North Berkshire photographer, with a studio at 48, Market Place and one also in Abingdon. He was the son of a draper in Wallingford Street, on the site of the present Waitrose, and became a professional photographer at the age of 21. He gained a reputation for all types of photography, views, family groups, children and animals.

Market Place, c. 1909. A Tom Reveley view of the Market Place, capturing a wide expanse of the area. Arthur Belcher is selling cycles. Bromley & Co have sheetings and calicoes displayed outside their shop. Traders habitually placed their goods outside shops in the nineteenth and early twentieth centuries and in Wantage the Commissioners continually requested that the pavements should be kept clear.

Shooting Party Lockinge, c. 1910. Lady Wantage (second from right) had regular 'shoots' This group could be a weekend house party, with the Prince of Wales present, who was to become George V. This is another Tom Reveley photograph. Among other royal visits to Lockinge House, recorded with his camera, were the Prince and Princess of Wales (Edward VII and Queen Alexandra), Edward VIII, when Prince of Wales, and his brother, the Duke of York, who was to become George VI.

A British Bulldog, c. 1905. Bromley Crib, one of the bulldogs photographed by Tom Reveley. Interestingly his pictures of bulldogs were produced for a 'Rotary Photographic Series' popular with Victorian and Edwardian postcard collectors and present day collectors will now pay as much as £4 or £5 for an original of these cards. Lord Wantage's famous shire stallion, 'Prince William' was photographed by him for Princess Alexandra, who was so delighted with the enlargement she decided to hang it in the hall at Sandringham.

BROMLEY CRIB.

25

MARKET PLACE, WANTAGE 12280

The North East Corner, c. 1912. The International Stores have tea chests stacked outside. H C Morse, House Agent & Auctioneer is next door, then Wheeler Bros tailors. F Chamberlain, hairdresser and photographer is in the Crown Inn building. Tom Reveley's new house has replaced Thatchers, and Valentine & Barrell have a hardware/clothing shop at the entrance to Wallingford Street. The cottages in Wallingford Street provided many homes. Clearly seen at the entrance to Newbury Street is Mr A V Gibbs, Music Stores and Printing Office, he was also agent for the North Berks Herald. Owners of businesses lived above or behind their shops. Accommodation for apprentices and domestic servants being provided on the top floor.

The Market Place, c. 1914. The Printing Office is prominent on early postcards. Mr Henry Nichols purchased the printing office in 1875, he was a correspondent for the North Wilts Herald and published a Nichols' Directory of Wantage for 38 years. The business was continued after his death by his son, Mr J A Nichols. To the left of this shop, Hiltons Booterie, London Central Meat Co, Fred Jackson, a butcher and Cottrell's fish shop.

The Market Place, c. 1909. This photograph shows more clearly the shops to the right of the Printing Office. W Castle, seed merchant and fruiterer in the shop advertising Cadbury's chocolate and to the right H Robins pharmaceutical chemist and Agency for Alliance Assurance, Fire, Life and Accident.

VC Gallery and Arbery, c. 1909. When the Victoria Cross paintings were being exhibited in the gallery a caretaker, George Hillier, was employed. Visitors had to ring a bell at the end of the passage, the admission charge 3d. The Hall was available for hire by the Community. The Arbery building to the left has been a draper's or mercer's business since the 17th Century and was bought around 1894 by J N Arbery, a silk mercer and draper from Wellington, Somerset.

Arbery, c. 1920. Howard Arbery, in the doorway, J N Arbery's son, took over the business in 1920, after serving in the Royal Flying Corps in WWI. The exterior has remained the same over the years, an excellent example of a Victorian shop with 'barley sugar' posts at the window corners. Cracks appeared in the front wall as a result of heavy military traffic during WWII or local quarrying. When the wall was repaired John Betjeman watched keenly to ensure the patterned bricks were replaced correctly.

Two

Events in the
Market Place

Church Parade, c. 1910. Church parades were an annual occurrence at this period. The Ardington Band, Wantage Fire Brigade and Boy Scouts are awaiting the arrival of soldiers of the Berkshire Yeomanry and Royal Berkshire Regiment for the band to play the troops to church. Elaborate Edwardian hats are evident; the milliners in the town made beautiful creations, even the babies have pretty bonnets. The chemist in the shop on the right is Mr Robins.

The Market, c. 1910. The charter for a market was granted by Henry III. During the last century the corn market was held on Wednesdays and meat, poultry, butter and vegetables sold on Saturdays. Farmers gathered regularly to buy and sell animals. In 1897 the Board of Agriculture ordered that all markets for the sale of pigs must be surfaced with gravel. The Council decided that bricks should be laid and an area was selected west of the statue for this purpose. The tender for the work executed by Mr W A Wheeler was £50.10s.3d. These bricks became known as the 'pig pavement'.

The Market (3) Wantage

Unveiling of the King Alfred Statue, 14 July, 1877. A wet day in Wantage, but this did not prevent the crowds arriving to witness the unveiling of the statue in the Market Place by the Prince and Princess of Wales, later to become Edward VII and Queen Alexandra. A dais was erected for the royal party and the band of the Grenadier Guards were in bright scarlet uniforms. The Wantage Volunteer Corps, under the command of Captain Brooks and Lieutenant Allen, formed a guard of honour. Children from the National and private schools were assembled, all wearing hats! (The children of Charlton School had to learn the song 'God Bless the Prince of Wales' and Mrs de Vitre from Charlton House provided the hats for them.) The royal visitors were met at Wantage Road Station by Colonel Loyd-Lindsay and escorted to the Market Place by a troop of the Berkshire Yeomanry. Mr H de Vitre accepted the gift of the statue for the town and read an address to the Prince of Wales. The Prince drew a cord to release the blue and white material covering the statue and declared it unveiled, 'amidst cheers and the playing of the National Anthem'. The Prince and Princess of Wales each planted a lime tree and then left to spend the weekend at Lockinge House as guests of Colonel and the Hon Mrs Loyd-Lindsay.

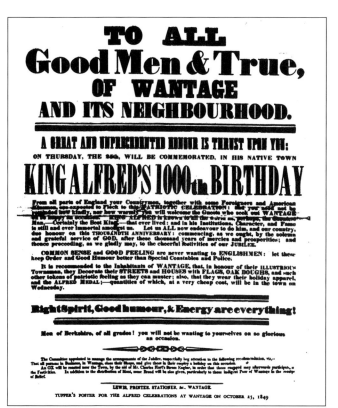

Celebration of the millenary of King Alfred's Birth, 25 October, 1849. This celebration was organised by Martin Tupper, a Victorian writer. A service was held in the Parish Church and a lecture on King Alfred in the Town Hall. At a dinner in the King Alfred's Head it was suggested that the old grammar school be revived and enlarged under the title of King Alfred's College. Mr Hart, owner of the iron works, provided a steam engine to turn the spit at an ox-roast. The ox fed 600 poor people.

Triumphal Arch, 14 July, 1877. Decorative arches were erected on roads to be travelled by the Prince and Princess of Wales during their visit to Wantage. Six members of the Berkshire Yeomanry in full dress uniform kept guard at the entrance to Newbury Street. The pond, enclosed by iron railings, is on the left. The Music Warehouse seen here was run by William G Gibbs and next door was A Winter, 'fancy' stationer.

Queen Victoria's Golden Jubilee, 1887. The day began with a procession to the Parish Church, where a service was held for all denominations. A free dinner was provided in the Market Place for nearly one thousand people and was followed by a children's tea. The children had to sing for their tea! They sang, 'Our Federated Empire', 'Our Empress Queen' and 'God Save the Queen'. They were presented with medals by Mr S W Silver. Sports and games were organised and bonfires illuminated the surrounding countryside in the evening.

Military Funeral of Lieutenant Napier Burnett Lindsay, 1909. Lieutenant Lindsay was killed in a hunting accident at Aldershot on 11 February. A special train ran from Aldershot to Wantage Road station, the couplings were slackened and the Tramway Company provided an engine to pull the main carriages to the Lower Yard at Wantage. The mill owners agreed not to use the yard for this day for goods transport.

The Berkshire Yeomanry, August 1914. Watched by a large number of people, 'D' Squadron mobilised at Wantage before joining the 2nd South Midland Brigade at Reading. This squadron consisted of the whole of the North Berks Yeomanry and numbered 120, all mounted. Each man was issued with 100 rounds of ammunition. They served in Egypt, Palestine and Gallipoli, during the First World War.

Commandeering Horses and Waggons, August, 1914. Farm waggons and horses being examined for transport purposes as part of the war effort. Mr Chamberlain, from the hairdresser and tobacconist shop, recalled seeing them and commented that many were shire horses and that these would have been used in 'Echelon B', as transport animals for the 'D' Squadron of the Berkshire Yeomanry. Shops illustrated are Hughes, boots and shoes, Chamberlain's, in the old Crown Inn, Tom Reveley's studio and Valentine & Barrell.

Armistice Celebrations, November 1918. News of the signing of the Armistice was posted in the Post Office. Flags appeared in the town and a special united thanksgiving service held. A huge bonfire was built in the Market Square which, when lit, burnt through the whole of the night. Hundreds of faggots and tar barrels were consumed.

Peace Celebrations, July 1919. The official day for celebrating peace was Saturday, 19 July. A competition for the best decorated tradesmen's carts was judged in the Market Place. Demobilised men, women and children gathered around the statue and, led by a band, sang the National Anthem. A message from the King was read by Mr J Welch the Town Crier. The band headed a procession to Stirlings Meadow, where sports were held and tea provided.

The Fair, 1910. Fairs in the Market Place have become more ambitious and noisier in recent years. In 1795 the fairs were held on the first Saturdays in March and May for horses and pedlary, on 17 July, for horses, pedlary and cherries and on 18 October for horses, pedlary, cheese, hops and hiring servants. The takings for the evening for this gentle roundabout ride were generously donated to the fund for the new steam fire engine. The firemen are lined up in appreciation of the gesture. Shadrach Bedford is on the left in the peaked cap.

Coronation of George V, June 1911. A successful celebratory day for the town. A committee was formed to organise the festivities, which included Messrs Robson, Kent, Castle, Candy, Noble, Aldworth and Arbery, with support from townspeople and businesses. The tradesmen's floats formed a procession from the Market Place down Wallingford Street, Garston Lane and Grove Street. Mr J N Arbery won first prize for the best decorated premises. In the afternoon sports were held on Stirlings Meadow.

Opposite: Cinematograph Entertainment, June 1912. Mr R S Lay (sixth from left), booked the VC Gallery for film shows on Thursday, Friday and Saturday every week for 6 months at a charge of £3 for the three nights, inclusive of gas and hall keeper's fees. He asked that a lamp be erected at the entrance and a lamp was removed from the north wall of the passage to the west wall to improve lighting.

The Coronation of George VI and Queen Elizabeth, 1937. A day of celebration in the Market Place. The bandstand is immediately behind the ox roast. Note the fashionable real fox fur, on the lady's shoulder. It is a cold day and there are not many customers for the 'stop me and buy one', selling tubs at 4d, choc bars 3d, brickettes 2d and snofrutes 1d. The fire was lit at midnight by Mr George Collier and Mr Freddie Fox, a jockey from Letcombe Regis. The ox was paraded from the Town Hall while the band played 'The Roast Beef of Old England'. When it was cooked, slices of meat were given out in sandwiches. No less than 3,456 halfpint cartons of beer were distributed. The King's speech was broadcast in the Market Place and then a confetti battle began.

Three
People of Wantage

Post Office Staff, 1908. This building in Newbury Street became a Post Office in 1900 and Mr W Wood was Postmaster. By 1912 the postmaster was Mr F Coombs. In 1793 Wantage had a postal delivery on only four days a week. William Wise bought the Fleur de Lys Inn (now Buckell & Ballard) in the nineteenth century and used the building behind for post. Later Joseph Lewis and then Alfred Deighton Clegg administered the post from Newbury Street.

Charabanc outing arranged by the Abingdon Arms, c. 1920. A message on this photograph reads, 'To bring back happy memories of the lovely day spent at the sea, only it was jolly wet. Got up at 4.30 am and arrived home at 12.30 am the next morning, having left Southampton at 8.30 pm'. The families from Grove Street are: Mr and Mrs Reeves, Mrs Major and Vera, Rose Pierpoint, Mrs Tarbois, Bill Gee, George Pierpoint, Flo and Ted Reeves, Mr and Mrs Beechey, Mrs and Sid Mulford, Mr and Mrs Gee, Gwen, George and Reg Gee, Mr and Mrs Haines, Mr Goodenough, Mr Hughes.

Fitting shop, Nalder & Nalder, c. 1925. Thomas Nalder founded this company at Challow, which produced portable engines and thrashing machines in the middle of the last century. The Company later progressed to making machinery for processing cocoa and coffee beans. Starting with the back row, left to right: Ernie Fulbrook, Tom Fleetwood, Jimmy Hammond, Eddie Fleetwood, Jack Moss, Charles Fleetwood, Charlie Lester, Frank Holder, Bert Jailes, Albert Kent, Sydney Rowland, -?-, Mickey Winterbourne, Bill Booker, Reg Cross, Bert Kent, -?-, Sydney Kent.

Bowling party, c. 1923. Bowling enthusiasts regularly met at houses with private greens. Here in the grounds of Brooklands, Newbury Street, Mr J N Arbery's home are, back row, left to right: Bertie Castle, Albert Stone Castle, James Dade (Lloyds Bank Manager), Joe Lyford, Toby Robson, -?-, Francis Pegler, 'Ossie's father'(!) from Walters the Jewellers, J N Arbery, J W Kent. In 1935 the Council resolved that an estimate be obtained for the construction of a bowling green in the Recreation Ground between the tennis courts and the Comrades' Club.

Wantage Team, Berks Constabulary Sports, July 1908. The victorious team was photographed behind the police station in Mill Street. In the tug-of-war final against Reading the team won the event on the first two pulls. Supt Smith captained the team consisting of P S Harris, PCs Barnard, Witt, Gunter, Couling, Hunter, Winchcombe and Walker. On their return to Wantage the tram was met at 'the crossing' by the Town Band and well-wishers who escorted them to the Market Place.

Church of England Boys' School, Newbury Street, c. 1928. Mr Gregory is the Master. In the second row from the back, second is Roy Hall, in the next row, fourth from left, Howard Lester, sixth, Cyril Prior, tenth, Aubrey Wood. Front row, second from left is Henry Mulford. Can you name any more of these young pupils?

Garston Lane Council School, 1937. Back row, left to right: Douglas Leahy, Frank Pullen, Stanley Payne, Sidney Gross, Roy Herring, Victor Beechey, George Westall. Second row: Reggie Winterbourne, Brian Lloyd, James Jakeman, Cissie Woolford, Joan Edwards, Ruby Bishop, Mavis White, Betty Comely, Amy Harris, Edwin Palmer, Bernard Simmonds, Arthur Harris. Third row: Roy Fox, Evelyn Collins, Irene Hemmings, Doreen Harris, Peggy Faulk, Gladys Brooks, Reggie Rumsby. Front row: Edward Harris, John Westmacott, Basil Prior, Peter Jefferies.

Alton House School, c. 1921. Mrs Edward Bayly founded a small private school in Newbury Street in about 1869, her daughter Caroline (sitting in the middle in this photograph) was still teaching the children of the business and farming community into the 1920s. This group was photographed in a garden in the Market Place. Sarah and Eileen Adkin (both in the second row from the back) joined Caroline as teachers, the rear of Messrs Adkin, Belcher & Bowen's premises was used for boarders.

King Alfred's Grammar School, c. 1910. A mixed age group of pupils, looking reasonably relaxed for this early photograph. They may have been boarders with the headmaster's wife.

Hospital Week, 1923. Friendly societies and other groups in the town organised events, including a tennis tournament and open air concert, to raise funds for the Cottage Hospital. This procession formed in the War Memorial Recreation Ground and after a parade around the town returned to Manor Road where a service was held. The Ardington Band led the procession with the Wantage Fire Brigade following. Mr Tom Roberts is riding on the horse-drawn steam fire engine (on the right), and the man in the trilby walking beside the band, is Mr A V Gibbs.

Wantage Fire Brigade, c. 1930. The new motorised fire engine is obscured by the firemen in this picture. Back row, left to right: Doug Belcher, Jim Wheeler, Albert Matthews, Arthur Collins, Jack Reeves, Len Hall, Bill Rogers, Ken Fleetwood. Front row: Bert Weston, Eben Reeves, Mr Arthur Gibbs, Tom Roberts, Laurie Pates. The firemen were originally called out with a siren, later bells were fitted in their houses.

Hospital Carnival, Engineering Company float, 1930. A Donkey Derby and Carnival was held in July of this year at The Ham, by kind permission of Mr and Mrs John Walters. This historic entry from the Engineering Company of blacksmith and welder, in the horse drawn tableau class, did not obtain a prize. The winner was Mr F E Smith of East Hendred with 'Speed the Plough, the farm through four seasons'.

Wantage Hospital Carnival, 6 July 1933. Carnivals had become a yearly event to raise money for the new hospital in Charlton Road. This tableau won first prize and was entered by T R Badger Ltd, Wallingford Street. The shop is on the left. From left to right: Gladys Wiltshire, Mary Badger, Mr A J Chandler, Cynthia Froude and Mary Rockall. Of interest also is Little Lane and the telephone exchange. Roberts Bros is on the right. The bricks in the lane (Rope lane) bore numbers used by the ropemakers to measure lengths of rope.

Wantage Engineering Company Sports and Fete, 1919. Company employees were given a holiday on full pay to attend these sports in a field at Charlton lent by Mr Chris Richens, to celebrate the signing of peace. The chairman of the committee was Capt C E Park MC (works manager) and Mr F Mulford, (standing third from left), the 'courteous and hardworking' Secretary. Lady Wantage, in the carriage, gave special prizes to the value of £10.00. About 3,000 people attended.

Wantage & District Farming Club, 1952. Farmers and their friends on a visit to Fort Dunlop. In the back rows group, left to right: Keith Hiskins, -?-, George Chandler, -?-, -?-, Brian Pocock, -?-, Ernie Chamberlain (Joe), -?-, Jack Cleaver and Herbie Church. Second row: -?-, Bertie Castle, Aubrey Pocock, Jim Pill, Jack Gosling, Michael Froud, Joe Hiskins (Theo), Edward Denley, Ted Froud, -?-. Front row: -?-, Aubrey Denley, Wilson Sharp, -?-, Edward Froud, Arthur Walford (Club Secretary), -?- and Stanley Pinnell.

Four

Wallingford Street, Charlton Road, Ormond Road

Messrs Valentine & Barrell Ltd, c. 1900. This is the half of the building that faced the Market Place, the remainder was in Wallingford Street. Traditionally much of the stock seems to be displayed outside and in the windows! On the left is Tom Reveley's house, he obtained permission from the Wantage Commissioners to build a studio behind here and facing North. Photographs are displayed, one of them is, inevitably, the King Alfred Statue.

Valentine & Barrell, c. 1900. Such a variety of goods outside in Wallingford Street, all had to be taken in at night but then labour was cheap. Mr T R Badger was apprenticed to the firm in Witney and in 1902 became manager of the Wantage branch. In 1908 the firm were making extensive alterations to adapt the premises to changing demands. On a Monday afternoon in 1908 the shop assistants were alarmed to hear falling mortar and see cracked ceilings, they ran into the street ...

Valentine & Barrell, c. 1908. The building collapsed. Beams, girders, bricks and debris soon covered and destroyed millinery, drapery, prams and furniture. Men climbed the ladders to remove the chimney which was leaning dangerously, a few vigorous blows from the ladder pushed the chimney into the yards behind the building with a tremendous crash. The china shop and the buildings in the Market Place were only slightly affected and business was resumed on the Wednesday.

Valentine & Barrell, c. 1908. The newly built shop in Wallingford Street. Mr T R Badger bought the business in 1915. Local people will be aware that his grandson continues the family tradition in Wantage with a men's outfitters at 21, Market Place.

Wallingford Street, c. 1915. Most of the buildings have vanished from this scene with the exception of those on the immediate right. Springfield Dairy, advertising teas, was run by Ernest Wilkins, he had a farm on Charlton Road. Subsequent owners were F Fitton and Mrs Wells. It became a general grocers and Frank Powles bought the business. Mr J S Trow the saddler and harness maker was succeeded by Mr E Barlow and Mr A S Brown. (see next page)

J. S. TROW,

SADDLER AND HARNESS MAKER.

HOME-MADE HARNESS A SPECIALITY.

Wallingford Street, WANTAGE,

BERKS.

Mr J S Trow, c. 1905. Mr W Howse was a saddler and harness maker in Wallingford Street and Mr G Wigmore in the Market Place.

Wallingford Street, c. 1918. An evocative photograph! These shops were demolished in the 1970s and replaced by a supermarket. The draper's shop was owned by Mr Roland Roberts, who when his wife died, asked his brother Tom to join him as a partner. Tom bought the premises from Mr Willis and the brothers were able to expand their business. Roland was a member of the Urban District Council for many years and Tom was a volunteer with the Wantage Fire Service and captain for seventeen years resigning in 1947.

Wallingford Street, c. 1920. Living accommodation for Mr and Mrs Tom Roberts and their young family was provided in the house on the left, which had three ground floor rooms, four bedrooms, attics and 'interesting outhouses'. The cottages on the right were demolished in the 1930s, the white building was U J Reeves & Sons, fish dealers and fish and chip shop, which survived. The surnames of the people living in the cottages were: Dowse, Delves, Huntley, Barkham and Cross.

Demolition of Wallingford Street cottages, c. 1935. Beer barrels form a convenient barrier. Mr Douglas Howse had a saddler's business and Miss Palmer a confectionery shop on the corner, both remained until after the Second World War. A shop was built on part of the site, called 'Mollie', which sold women's fashions in the 1950s.

Wallingford Street, c. 1940. The Home Guard marching towards the Market Place. The open space which had been the site of some of the cottages remained until the 1960s.

Wallingford Street, c. 1910. In 1891 Mrs Caudwell lived at The Ivies, the house on the left with the brick wall and iron gate, and Mr P Jones, photographer, had a small studio there in about 1920. 'D' Troop of the Berkshire Yeomanry met at the next house, still called the Old Yeomanry House. Rock Well brewery, the Queen Anne house facing down this street, had extensive grounds. Ingold and Lewis were the brewers.

Welcome Home to the troops, 1919. A wooden cross was carved and erected outside the old Rock Well brewery premises to be a shrine to the memory of the men who died in the 1914-18 War, and a focus for a march past. As a permanent memorial to the men who died a recreation ground in Manor Road was to be created for the community. It was decided to keep the wooden cross and permission was obtained for it to be sited in the Parish Churchyard.

Wallingford Street, c. 1910. Do you know where this photograph was taken? A clue is the brick wall. On the left are the grounds of Stirlings, to become 'Thermidor' and Haywards Close, on the right is St Katharine's School and in the distance is the brick wall surrounding the grounds of Charlton House and the site of the Wantage Hospital.

St Katharine's School, c. 1910. It was built in 1898 by the architect A N Mowbray. St Katharine's originated in Newbury Street, part of a 'middle' school run by the sisters of the Community of St Mary the Virgin. Its object was to give a better education to children than could be had at the national schools, with lower fees than St Mary's School. The day pupils were mostly daughters of local business men, it also became a boarding school, a kindergarten and preparatory school for boys and girls. In 1938 the school was amalgamated with St Helen's in Abingdon.

Thermidor, c. 1973. An unusual house for this area, built about 1930 by Mr Henry Thurston (of the Engineering Company) on the grounds which once belonged to Stirlings. The interior was furnished in the style of the period. It had a stark white appearance with net curtains at the windows. The house and grounds were eventually sold and the Hayward's Close houses built here. A unique photographic record captured just as the builders were moving in!

Wantage Cottage Hospital, c. 1930. In 1924 it was proposed that a new hospital be built, to replace the Belmont hospital. Mr A S Castle offered land in Ham Road and Mr A T Loyd promised £2,000 on condition that the hospital committee raised £4,000 by the end of the year. The sum of £8,000 was raised by the people of Wantage and surrounding villages. The land in Ham Road was considered unsuitable and a corner of the Charlton House grounds was acquired, Mr Castle donating £200. The new hospital was opened in 1927 by Princess Helena Victoria, the third daughter of Queen Victoria.

Ivy Cottage, c. 1913. This cottage stood facing the hospital until recently and is often, wrongly, considered to have been the turnpike house. The actual turnpike was on the opposite side of Ormond Road behind the house demolished to widen the cross roads. Mr and Mrs Seymour lived for years in Ivy Cottage with their nine children.

Charlton Road, c. 1914, photographed from the present hospital crossroads with the garden of Ivy Cottage on the right. The space between these Edwardian houses was bought for the new Roman Catholic Church. There is no pavement on the right and the weeds or ivy are trailing on to the road. On the left are the walled grounds of Charlton House.

Charlton Road, c. 1915. The hospital crossroads is in the distance. It is difficult to appreciate that this road had few houses during the previous century. Iron railings were widely used for fencing. Wantage, like many towns, had its own manufacturing facility in the local engineering company.

The Wantage Engineering Company, c. 1910. Early development of the company is attributed to Charles Hart, who became known for the manufacture of the Berkshire plough and threshing machines. Later owners included Messrs Gibbons, and Robinson and Auden, who manufactured agricultural machines, engines and steam driven waggons, and traded as the Vale of White Horse Iron Works. Lord Wantage bought the company in 1900. George Thurston took over the controlling interest in 1917, producing mining equipment for export.

Ormond Road, c. 1920. On the right is Hildon House, attached to the engineering works, known to local people as The Foundry. Early owners lived in this house. The Three Pigeons public house was situated past the car on the right, the road formerly called Three Pigeons or Foundry Lane. Horse and motor transport are seen competing here in the twenties. An example of the distinctive chequered Wantage brickwork can be seen on the left. These houses were demolished to build Partridge Close.

Foundry Villas, c. 1910. Looking towards Ormond Road, where a general store and sweet shop was conveniently situated. The grandly named 'Villas' were built to house foundry employees. These houses were demolished to build homes for the elderly which were given the name of Three Pigeons Close.

Almshouse Close, c. 1904. The Christmas Fat Stock Show, a big event for all local farmers and well supported by them with a permanent committee. This is now the site of the fire and ambulance stations in Ormond Road. The Eagles almshouses in the background were built in 1867, costing upwards of £1,100. They are administered by the Governors of Town Lands.

Ormond Road, c. 1915. In the distance are new Edwardian or late Victorian houses. The traditional patterned bricks of the town can be seen on the houses on the right. A primitive footpath on the left leads into St Katharine's School. Is the bucket about to be used to pick up the horse manure? - it was a prized fertiliser for gardens.

Orchard Way, c. 1935. These 'council' houses in Wantage are attractive and well spaced. In 1919, fifty houses were built; thirty six at West Hill and fourteen at Garston Lane. In 1932 forty houses were built on four acres of land in Orchard Way. This building followed the house clearance programme of the 1930s to provide essential new homes.

Five
Church Street, Priory Road, Newbury Street, Portway

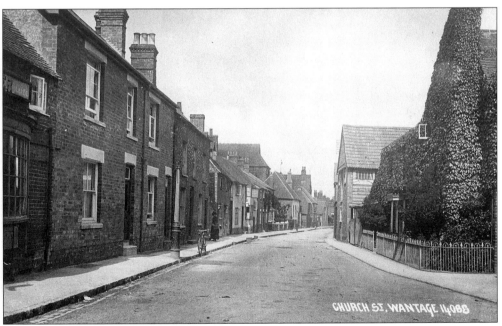

Church Street, c. 1910. At the end of the nineteenth century this street was known as Back Street. Mr J Whiting, the builder, occupied the barn on the right and also arranged funerals. The buildings in the distance, the Three Tuns public house, a brewery and the church hall have now all vanished to make way for the police station, court and a car park.

Church Street, c. 1912. The photographer is standing outside what is now the museum, looking towards the house occupied by Wantage doctors for many years. Mr J Kent, builder, lived and worked from buildings on the left. The impressive lime trees were felled when suspected of being diseased.

The Vicarage, c. 1914. On arriving in Wantage in 1846 the Revd William Butler was disheartened to find a very dilapidated Elizabethan vicarage. He asked George Edmund Street to design a new vicarage, which was built in 1850. Street, a young Tractarian architect, lived in Wallingford Street. Near the end of his life he was chosen as the architect to design the new Law Courts in London but did not live long enough to see the finished building.

Church of St Peter and St Paul, c. 1914. A thirteenth century church which has undergone rebuilding over the centuries. Despite early opposition in the town the Revd Butler employed George Street to restore the chancel. High pews and galleries were removed and a new pulpit designed in 1857. In 1881 the nave was lengthened by one bay westward and the south porch moved, the architect, William Butterfield, who also designed the font cover. The iron railings were removed for the 1939-45 war effort. The lower picture shows an area devoid of graves where a Norman church and Latin School stood until 1850. The Governors of Town Lands maintained a schoolmaster to teach 'Gramer within the said Town of Wantinge'. The wooden memorial, used as a focus for the Peace Celebrations in 1919, remained a memorial here until 1948.

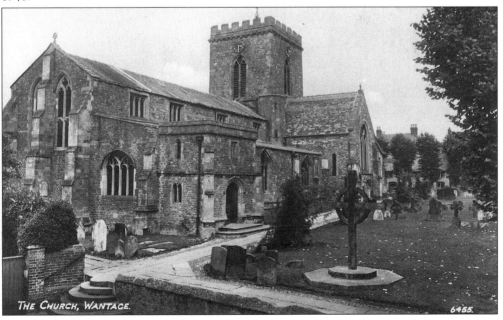

Home Guard Band, c. 1942. Capt H A Glaysher was the Battalion Adjutant from January 1942 to February 1945, seen here leading the band for a Remembrance Day Service. They are lined up in Church Street near Dr F V Squires' house. George Payne organised the band with some members from the old Lockinge and Ardington Bands.

Priory Road, c. 1949, one of the oldest streets in Wantage. The Adkin Memorial Hall for the Girl Guides replaced cottages at the end. It was known for many years as Tanner Street, after the homes of the tanners on the left. The grape vine is still in existence. Further down on the left in the grandest house of the row lived Philip Allen, the owner of the tanyard.

St Michael's School and Chapel, c. 1900. The school was built by Mrs Trevelyan in 1855, the architect was Wm. White. She had already founded a school for the training of young girls for domestic service at Littlemore which she transferred to Wantage. Children were sent from the National Schools as young as nine years old. To further education in the area the Revd Butler persuaded Mrs Trevelyan to add a school for the training of pupil teachers and the Sisters of the Wantage Community became more involved in the work. The Apsidal was added to the Chapel in 1888, the architect was A B Allin. St Michael's has been converted to private residences and the chapel is now part of an apartment.

Newbury Street, c. 1920. The house on the left was the London County and Westminster Bank. On the immediate right is Clegg & Son, chemists and printers and J H May, draper, the premises were called Bon Marché. The shop facing is also called Clegg & Son, 'Oil & Color Stores'.

Newbury Street, c. 1912. The Ardington Stores carriage may be parked for loading or perhaps it is purchasing ale not sold in the Boar's Head at Ardington, which became a temperance house in Lord Wantage's time. This postcard was sent to Master J Trinder from his cousin Jack, who is standing in the road in this picture with 'one of his chum messengers'. Jack had just passed examinations to become a postman.

The Wesleyan Church, c. 1910, was built of rag stone with Bath stone dressings and erected in 1844 at a cost of £1,271 14s 5d. A building at the rear was a Sunday and day school where the fees were 2d, 3d and 6d per week, according to the class to which the scholar belonged. The poster is advertising a Men's Meeting on Sundays from 3-4 pm.

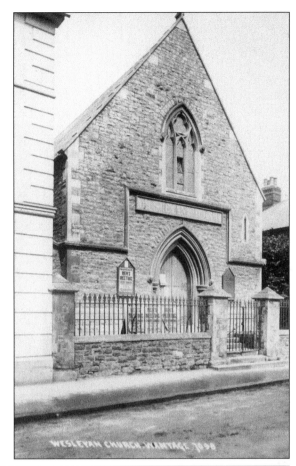

Newbury Street, c. 1910. Tubb's House, (now the Art Block for St Mary's School), heavily covered in ivy. Tubbs and Stirlings, both demolished were considered to be two eighteenth-century houses worth seeing in Wantage. Next door is an extension for the school designed by the architect William Butterfield in 1874. St Anne's opposite also became part of the school.

Newbury Street, Wantage

St Mary's School, c. 1906. The school developed from a small middle school for girls housed in the Georgian building on the far side of the chapel in this photograph, an early home of the sisters of the Community of St Mary the Virgin. It became a boarding school 'for the daughters of gentlemen, clergy and professional men' and was staffed by the sisters. The chapel was built in fancy gothic style by the architect, Ponting.

Newbury Street, c. 1910. The majority of the cottages on the left have disappeared, only one remains next to the Royal Oak. The present garage trading here evolved from the small shop selling cycles and motor spares. Gradually the small cottages were swallowed up to provide garage facilities for the new motor owners.

The Royal Oak, c. 1920. An indenture of 1767 between John Winkworth, sackcloth weaver and Edward Evans, hempdresser, which leased the Royal Oak of Newbury Street for seven years gives an indication of the age of, at least, the rear part of the public house. The name was derived from the episode when Charles II hid in an oak tree to escape capture, but is now in honour of the battleship of the same name.

Portway Place, c. 1912. Mr L J Lloyd, wheelwright and coach builder, lived on the left. The horse and cart belonged to a grocer and baker. Mr Lloyd was aware of the implications of the changes that were takng place in transport, from horses to motor cars, and adapted his skills accordingly. On the right, in Portway Terrace, lived Mrs L Hiskins from the Wharf and further along Mr E T W Nalder owned Orchard House, the house bought by the Urban District Council to replace the Town Hall.

King Alfred's Grammar School, c. 1916. Following the celebrations of the millenary of King Alfred's birth, it was suggested that a suitable method of commemorating the event would be the rebuilding of the Grammar School, and on a more suitable site. It was built of Cirencester stone with Bath stone quoins and dressings by the architect, J B Clacy. The corner stone was laid by Mr B Wroughton in July 1850. The doorway from the Norman church and Elizabethan school in the churchyard was restored and incorporated into the schoolroom. The 'new School Room', with distinctive brick architecture, at the rear of the playground, was built in 1872, the architect was William Butterfield. Later the North Wing and dormitories were added and the headmaster's house enlarged.

Letcombe Fields, c. 1910. This scene is perhaps not so easily recognised as the path to Letcombe is now fenced. Near King Alfred's School, the Letcombe Fields were a convenient spot to settle disputes between the Town boys and the School boys.

Ickleton Road, c. 1910. This view is easily recognisable, with the bridge over the Letcombe Brook. A plaque was affixed on the side of this bridge which reads 'On 3rd August 1901 in a nearby meadow a group of campers led by T H Holding founded the Camping Club of Great Britain and Ireland.' The lodge for The Ham is on the left.

The Ham, c. 1910. This early Georgian house was owned by Mr John Price during the eighteenth century. Price's colourful and interesting map of Priorshold, now deposited in Shire Hall, bears a sketch of the original building. An inventory of the contents of the house sold in 1782 lists '1 case with Map of Mannor in the Weighting Room'.

Alma House, Newbury Street, c. 1910, was probably named in commemoration of Colonel Robert Loyd-Lindsay's part in the victory at the Battle of the Alma in the Crimean War, for which he obtained the Victoria Cross. The front door has now been bricked up and the elaborate porch removed. The house is part of St Mary's School.

Newbury Street, c. 1940. These are typical houses of the town, patterned bricks on the right and blue glazed bricks on the left. Army vehicles are parked outside Brooklands, which suggests it was photographed at the beginning of the Second World War.

Stiles Almshouses, c. 1960. Mr Robert Stiles of Amsterdam died in 1680 and in his will he left farm and lands at Andover, the proceeds of which were to be used to build twelve almshouses and pay for their maintenance. The houses were built around a courtyard and the the entrance passage was paved on each side with the knuckle bones of sheep - a reminder of the old industries of the town.

Six

Mill Street, Camel, Belmont, Grove Street

Mill Street, c. 1910. Henry George Mulcock, hairdresser: perfumier and tobacconist, 'hair brushed by machinery', Park Drive cigarettees, ten for 2d! The Baptist Church was built in 1860 at a cost of £1,450 and seated 250 people. The garage on the corner has progressed from cycles to motor cars and has an appropriate entrance for the vehicles. The petrol pumps were attached to the wall and swung over the road to fill cars with fuel.

Mill Street, c. 1915. P W Belcher's Tea Stores is remembered for its enticing aroma of freshly roasted coffee beans. Two doors up is a butcher's shop, possibly that of Mr E C Allee. The Tramway Office is resplendent with a new frontage. Mr W A Noble was Manager and Mr J Bullock, Goods Manager.

Mill Street, c. 1915. On the left the Church Reading Room, this was preceded by a Reading Room in the Town Hall and in Church Street. It was open all day and in the evenings, providing newspapers and a library, a billiard room upstairs. Chess competitions were held. The passage is the entrance to the Diamond Jubilee Swimming Bath. The almshouses on the right were built in three stages, 1868, 1870 and 1871 and replaced earlier dilapidated houses. They are administered by the Governors of the Town Lands, a body set up in 1597.

The Shears, c. 1910. A photograph taken just before the old Shears Inn was replaced by a new version in 1912. Rock Well Brewery are advertised as the brewers, Mr E Manuel of the Shears in 1912 was also a blacksmith. A boot and shoe maker worked in the part of the building next to the Mill Stream. There is an interesting example of ivy cultivation on the houses on the left.

The Lamb, c. 1920. The Lamb is newly thatched and has windows at the extreme end. Mr F B Pittaway of the Lamb was also a baker and confectioner. The ivy covered police station on the right has a typical station lamp outside. The Jolly Waterman and wharf cottages in the distance were eventually considered unfit for habitation and demolished.

The Mill, c. 1920. This was originally used as an office and store for the operational mill on the brook. It was conveniently sited for the lower yard of the tramway and for the transportation of grain and flour for Mr Percy Clark of the Mill. When Messrs W H Munsey Ltd of Osney Mills bought the mill in 1948, this building was converted into a working mill and is producing flour at the present time. The old mill over the brook has been divided into residential apartments.

The German Gun, c. 1919. After the First World War, German guns were distributed to towns as war trophies. This gun, a 106 mm Howitzer and carriage was placed in the Market Place by the Town Property Committee. When news of the peace being signed reached Wantage, flags were displayed and fireworks let off. A crowd gathered in the Market Place and a group of discharged men rushed to the gun and, using ropes, manhandled it down Mill Street and into the stream. It remained there until 1921.

Mill Street, c. 1920. Mill Street was often flooded. The water of Letcombe Brook was a very powerful stream and powered three mills as it ran through Wantage. Here the flood water is gushing out of the stream in front of the mill. Note the sign of the Shears public house, up on the wall, an indication of the cloth making in the town. It has been moved to the side of the new building.

Reeves & Son, Fish and Chip Cafe, c. 1948. Previously Goddard's fruit and vegetable shop, and a 'wet fish' shop, until Ted and Jack Reeves opened their cafe here. It opened on Mondays, Tuesdays and Thursdays at 5 pm, Fridays and Saturdays at 11.30 am. No frozen ready to cook pieces of fish in those days! The fish was collected from Wantage Road Station at about 8.15 am, gutted and prepared for frying. Batter had to be mixed and potatoes chipped. Unfortunately, it suffered the same fate as the Wharf houses and was eventually demolished.

Mill Street, c. 1932. Blenheim Garage is in the distance on the left, previously Blenheim Orchard, named after a variety of apple grown there. The Bellinger family were owners of the garage for sixty years. The petrol pumps advertised the brand of petrol at the top and were illuminated at night. The site has recently been developed for housing. Mr John Pates, a coal merchant, hired out sacks from the wooden building. The iron gates marked the entrance to Littleworth House where the Pinnock brothers, Stan and Hubert, lived.

The Camel, c. 1915. The view has not changed, but the method and speed of transportation on this road is so different. The new stone wall encloses the Convent built on the corner of Denchworth and Faringdon Roads. The Camel public house stood on the cross roads, and at the beginning of the 1800s achieved notoriety for bullbaiting.

St Mary's Home, c. 1907. The Community of St Mary the Virgin was founded by the Revd William Butler. The Wantage Sisters, a community of three or four women, started their work in the parish under Elizabeth Lockhart, in cottages in Newbury Street, now St Mary's School. Although William Butler wished them to be primarily concerned with visiting the poor and female education, a penitentiary was formed here at the insistence of Archdeacon Henry Manning.

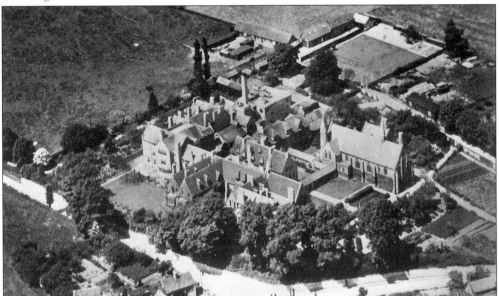

St Mary's Convent, c. 1934. The foundation stone was laid for St Mary's Home in 1854, the sisters moving into their new home in 1856. Designed by George Street, it was built in local limestone. The chimney stacks formed decorative features. Street was also the architect for St Mary Magdalene's Chapel, built in 1866. The larger chapel, St Mary's, was designed by J L Pearson in 1877. The Community has branch houses and sisters from the order have worked in India since as long ago as 1877 and in South Africa since 1902.

Denchworth Road, c. 1900. The road from Barwell to Grove, a quiet agricultural part of Wantage. Farms existing in this area were Barwell, Stockham and Belmont. There were also nurseries at Belmont.

Opposite: The Cottage Hospital Grounds, 1911. The Cottage Hospital was administered by a Committee and supported generously by local people. Regular gifts of food were presented and yearly hospital carnivals and processions organised by friendly societies and tradespeople raised money.

The Cottage Hospital, Belmont, 1905. Mr Percy Smith of Letcombe Bassett died in 1883 and in his will bequeathed £5,000 'to be applied in the establishment and maintenance of a cottage hospital for the poor and sick inhabitants of Wantage and neighbourhood'. The trustees were his wife Susannah and Messrs Jotcham and Marlow, who were prohibited from spending any part of the money on the building. A new house in Belmont was purchased with public subscription and furnished by Mrs Silver of Letcombe Regis.

Cottage Hospital Grounds, Wantage

Grove Street, c. 1910. Mr W Cooper had a greengrocer's shop in this timber-framed seventeenth-century building. The lane led to Falcon Court and the gates to the back entrance of the Town Hall. The Revd William Butler was always concerned about living conditions in Grove Street and through his work as Town Commissioner facilitated many improvements.

Grove Street, c. 1908. Few early photographs exist of Grove Street. In the eighteenth century Brian's Brook ran through the street at the bottom of the hill and a prosperous tannery stretched out through Stirling's Lane on the left. In 1829 the owner became bankrupt and all the tan pits and buildings connected with the tannery were removed. Note the sarsen stone on the side of the road, to protect the adjacent building from damage by cart wheels. The Clock House, through the gap on the left (not visible in this picture) was the home of the owner of the rope works.

Grove Street, c. 1919. The 1920s and 1930s brought prosperity to Grove Street, shops and businesses were flourishing. William Massey occupied the prominent shop on the right, Albert Meilke, a grocer was at No 5. Albert Thornhill was a newsagent at No 19 and Frederick Simmons, a farmer from Belmont Farm, had a dairy at No 21.

Grove Street, c. 1910. The building on the right was Bennett's Brewery; 'F H Bennett, wine, spirit and hop merchant'. People with a variety of trades and professions lived in the street: G Reeves, pork butcher, Tom Richings and A W Shepherd, bakers and Shadrach Bedford was a whitesmith, locksmith, bell hanger and gas fitter. S G Summerhayes, a solicitor's clerk, Hedley Long, a schoolmaster and J A Godwin, a trainer, all lived in the street at this time.

The Elms, c. 1908. When Miss Martha Liddiard died her 'villa residence' was bought by Mr Thomas Clark, in 1883, for £1,000, which included 3 acres of land. Elm Cottages were also sold as an investment, the rent producing £94 per annum. This postcard was used as a Christmas card by Mr and Mrs Thomas Clark. The house was sited where the Ridgeway garage now operates.

Seven

Brookside and Lock's Lane

The Town Mill, c. 1910. A mill has existed on this site since the time of the Domesday Book. Mr James Clark owned the mill, and subsequently, his son Thomas Clark and grandson Percy Clark. In 1908 a company was formed, Clark's Wantage Ltd. The mill specialised in milling English wheat and its products were conveyed using the tramway.

Brookside Cottages, c. 1930. These cottages were condemned in the 1930s and eventually demolished and the inhabitants rehoused. The water in the brook was often badly polluted, with treated effluent from the sewage works, as well as domestic waste, discharged straight into the stream. The Iron Bridge can be seen in the distance which was erected in 1859 at a cost of £41.00.

The Iron Bridge, c. 1909. The Vicar of Wantage (1847-1880), the Revd Canon Butler, recorded in his diary for Ascension Day 1871, 'Coming home at night I found the iron bridge filled with young men. This is a great evil. They make unpleasant remarks to girls and others passing by. I spoke to them about this and as they did not seem inclined to move I took out my Prayer book, read the Gospel for Ascension Day and preached them a short sermon. This answered well, I wished them good night and as I entered my garden they all walked away, responding to me in a very friendly tone.'

Brookside Cottages, c. 1910. At the beginning of the century at the side of the brook and past the iron bridge, there was an orchard on the right, then two groups of cottages. The group on the left was built on a piece of land referred to in John Price's map of 1754 as 'The Gogs'. Here the water is diverted in front of the houses, under the Platt Bridge and down to Mill Street. The path at the side of this water course to Mill Street has always been known to Wantagians as The Gogs.

The Platt Bridge, 1910. A closer and picturesque view of the cottages. In 1925 two houses were flooded at Brookside. The houses had water in the lower rooms to a depth of nine inches, the occupants having to live in the upper rooms. The path to the left leads to Lock's Lane, the Platt footpath ahead to Ham Road. The field on the left is part of The Mead grounds and Mr Clark's orchard was on the right.

The Mead, c. 1907, was, for many years, the home of cloth makers, the Hazell family. Lord Wantage bought the small estate 'known as The Mead, containing the petrifying spring called King Alfred's Bath' in 1871. The poet Sir John Betjeman owned the property from 1946 until 1972.

The Mead Path, c. 1907. Sir John Betjeman walked to the parish church alongside the Letcombe Brook at Wantage. In the church tower is the manuscript of a poem he composed entitled Wantage Bells, the first verse reads :

Now with the bells through the apple bloom
Sundayly sounding
And the prayers of the nuns in their chapel gloom
Us all surrounding,
Where the brook flows
Brick walls of rose
Send on the motionless meadow the bell notes rebounding...

'Factory Buildings', c. 1918. In early maps this area is shown as having factory buildings, probably for the manufacture of cloth. It has been fenced differently in later years and this part of the brook is now within a private garden. Barns are visible in the gardens of the houses in front of the church.

The Mead Path, c. 1908. The countryside within Wantage, the Mead path from Lock's Lane to Platt Bridge. The factory buildings and church can be seen on the left and St Michael's School on the right. The loss of some trees and the growth of others gives quite a different view in 1995.

Willoughby's Mill and Ford, c. 1910. An old Wantage family, the Willoughbys, owned this mill for at least 200 years. Robert Willoughby was the miller in 1793. In the 1930s the original mill stones were still in use and until 1929 the mill was driven by a sixteen ft, Brestshot water wheel. It was then a grist mill, grinding food for animals. Mr Geoffrey Willoughby died tragically in the mill in 1944. He was a councillor, a staunch member of the Oddfellow Friendly Society and served with the Royal Field Artillery in the First World War.

Lock's Lane, c. 1910. The lane from Ham Road to Priory Road was named after Thomas Lock, who was fined for letting his pigs stray in the lane. On the left the water runs down from Alfred's Bath, on the right is a barn in the grounds of the Mill House.

Alfred's Bath, c. 1900. When Lord Wantage purchased King Alfred's Bath, it was expected that it would be made 'a place of great beauty'. This early photograph shows it as a Victorian/Edwardian beauty spot. The area was normally locked and anyone wishing to visit it had to obtain a key from a neighbouring house. The Bath was given to the town and the Urban District Council assumed responsibility for maintenance but it has been neglected since the Second World War.

Eight
The Wantage Tramway

Wantage Road Station, c. 1919. The need to choose a route for the Great Western Railway as free as possible from severe gradients and expensive engineering works left Wantage $2\frac{1}{2}$ miles to the South of the nearest halt. Proposals for a branch line did not receive support from local business people.

The Hughes tram engine with cars 3, 1 and 4 approaching Grove Bridge, c. 1910. The construction of the tramway resulted from a meeting held on 22 October 1873, chaired by Lt Col Loyd-Lindsay VC MP (to become Lord Wantage). The proposal to link Wantage and Wantage Road Station with a horse powered tramway at the side of the road met with enthusiastic support from local people. A Limited Liability Company was formed and £3,000 was immediately subscribed in £5 shares.

Matthews' Tram Engine No 6, with car No 5, c. 1920. From its inception the promoters of the tramway had intended to operate the line by steam, approval was given in 1876, when Merryweathers Grantham car was put into service. The Matthews was built in 1880 and purchased by the company in 1888, at a cost of £60, as the Grantham was approaching the end of its useful life. It was withdrawn in 1925 when the passenger service ceased.

Manning & Wardle's Saddle Tank Engine, No 7, c. 1920 and considered to be the most successful engine the tramway possessed. A goods engine, purchased in 1893, costing about £300, which also hauled passenger cars. This was withdrawn in 1945 and sold when the tramway was dismantled.

Engine No 5, a George England Well Tank Engine, c. 1910, built in 1857 and purchased by the Tramway Company in 1878. Engines working on the tramway were usually given nicknames, No 5 was known as 'Jane'. In the early 1920s she regularly steamed sixty miles a day, carrying various goods but most often coal.

The Tramway Terminus and
Mill Street, Wantage.

Tramway Terminus, Mill Street, c. 1910. The office in Mill Street was completed in 1904. This new office formed an extension to the original station, a two storey building with the name of the line and the date on the front. The manager's office was upstairs, and the general office, containing timetables and travel guides, was on the ground floor. Passengers could pass from the Mill Street office, through the old station house and out on to the covered platform.

Matthews' Tram Engine waiting at the Tramway Terminus, c. 1914. The fares in 1923 were: Wantage to Wantage Road, 9d, to Grove Bridge, 3d and Oxford Lane, 6d. Competition from the motorbus led to closure of the passenger service; the motor bus fare to the station was only 6d. Comparing the two services, a resident commented to a journalist of the Chronicle, 'A ride on our tramway is the finest thing for the liver ever thought of. We scarcely need doctors in Wantage.'

Elms Cottages, Grove Road, c. 1911. The tramway line crossed Grove Road below Elms Cottages, a goods train can just be seen returning from Wantage Road. The cyclist is on the right hand side of the road, ready to cycle to the left, the rails would throw him if he attempted a straight ride over. This trick had to be remembered by all local cyclists.

The Hughes tram engine passing The Elms, c. 1910. Thomas Clark lived at The Elms and the train would sometimes stop here to pick up fruit from his orchard, destined for Covent Garden. In this picture the children are probably posed by the photographer in readiness for the passenger tram to pass by.

99

Engine No 7 at Grove Bridge, c. 1920. The tram has passed Elms Farm and reached Grove Bridge, where the road and tramway crossed the canal on separate bridges. Application had to be made by the Tramway Company to the Wilts & Berks Canal for permission to construct this additional bridge, a penalty of £100 was requested. The Driver is John Hewitt.

The Hughes Tram Engine returning to Wantage, c. 1915. The tram is about to cross the canal bridge. A passing loop was constructed at this point.

'Jane', Engine No 5, with passengers making a 'photographic stop', c. 1920. George Weaving, the driver, was employed by the company for 40 years.

The Hughes' Tram Engine, with cars 1 and 3, returning from Wantage Road Station, c. 1911. The bridge over the GWR line can be seen in the distance. The conductor for this trip, William Savory, was appointed at the age of thirty-one at 14s a week. He worked for the Tramway Company for 30 years and then became the caretaker at the Victoria Cross Gallery.

The Hughes' Engine at Grove Park Lodge, c. 1911. The entrance to the private road commissioned by Col Robert Loyd-Lindsay. This gave the Colonel and his family a quicker and more comfortable ride to the station and also quicker transport of goods and animals to and from Ardington and Lockinge.

The Matthews' Engine at Wantage Road Station, with car 6, c. 1912. The passenger service was arranged to connect with the stopping trains. The timetable for 1879 indicates seven trips daily, with eight on Wednesdays, Market Day. There was never a Sunday service. Luggage was carried on the platform at the end of the car and under the supervision of the conductor.

Tram Engine No 5, derailed, c. 1930. Although the journey to Wantage Road could be leisurely and uneventful, with branches of trees gently brushing against the car windows, derailments did occur. In the autumn of 1893 Mrs Pottinger was offered £2 in settlement of her claim for shock received when the tramcar got off the rails. In 1922 it was recorded that 'Jane' had smashed a motor car and a cart, killed a bullock and been off the track about six times!

Our Local Express, c. 1908. Martin Anderson (Cynicus), a prolific artist who set up his own company producing postcard designs. He dealt with many aspects of Edwardian life and the Wantage Tramway did not escape his attention and sense of fun.

Wantage Road Station, c. 1915. A simple station with long straight lines stretching out towards Swindon. The footbridge has yet to be built and people are walking across the lines to reach the other platform. Before Wantage Road became an official stopping place for trains, travellers to Wantage used Challow Station.

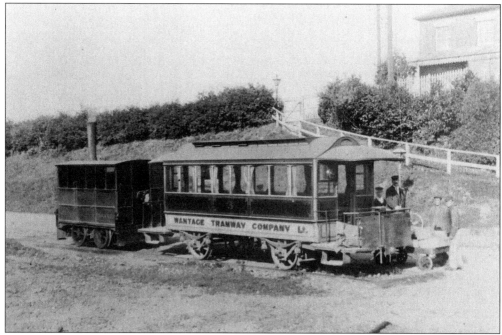

The Hughes' Tram Engine and car No 3 at Wantage Road Station nearly ready for the journey back to Wantage. The trams met all trains. Small goods could be carried on the platform, mail, meat, fish, papers, parcels. The signalman's house is on the right. The pathway leads to the Wantage-Oxford Road.

Nine
The Wilts & Berks Canal

Wantage Wharf, c. 1890s. The Wilts & Berks Canal was cut from the Kennet & Avon Canal at Semington, near Melksham, to the Thames at Abingdon from 1796 to 1810. An arm to Wantage left the main waterway West of Grove Top Lock terminating at this Wharf located at the base of Mill Street opposite the Town Mill. Water transport enabled the movement of heavy loads of stone, which became a popular material for new buildings in the town.

Wantage from the Canal, c. 1895. A peaceful length of water, much enjoyed for walking, fishing and pleasure boating. When frozen over in winter it was possible to skate to Abingdon jumping over the locks at Grove.

Opposite: Wantage Wharf and Basin, c. 1904. The basin and wharfinger's house can be seen in the distance and the canal is silting up. The GWR line from London to Bristol was opened in 1841. The salt trade and part of the coal trade was transferred to rail in 1873. The canal was described at this time by Mr Ormond as a 'muddy ditch', but was still carrying 2000 tons of coal in 1876 and 1878.

Wantage from the Wharf, c. 1900. Trade on the canal is ceasing, weed is flourishing and a narrow boat provides a platform for fishing. This is Wharf Terrace, a row of houses and the Jolly Waterman, the public house whose faggots were famous among the canal users, which were demolished in the 1970s.

Wharfinger's House and Narrow Boat, c. 1895. The Wharfinger's house with stables, the posts for entrance gates and the sack hiring shed also still exist (note that the latter is not visible in this photograph). The Hiskins family lived in the stone house and traded in coal, coke, salt, hay, straw and manure.

The Wharf Crane, c. 1900. This crane was subsequently sold to the Tramway Company. Ralph Hiskins used to reminisce on his boyhood spent close to the wide stretch of water which formed the Wharf. One of his favourite games with friends was to swing out over the wharf on the crane, if they didn't have enough momentum to carry them to the opposite bank, they made quite a splash!

Smallmarch or Spirit Lock, c. 1895. Albert Stone Castle, the main farmer in Charlton, sits proudly on the lock close to his land. The Grove flight consisted of six locks, Grove Bottom, Spirit, Smallmarch, Grove Common, Limekiln and Grove Top. In his diary entry of 1879 he was very concerned that the canal would freeze over and his order for manure would be delayed! The wide expanse of water could be the reservoir for filling and emptying the lock and a convenient mooring place for boats.

Looking towards Hunter's Bridge, 1904. This photograph from Stockham Bridge was taken by Miss Gregory in the Spring of 1904.

Ten

Charlton and Farming

Charlton, c. 1880. The villagers of Charlton were dependent on agriculture. The late enclosures of 1868 changed the village, the people losing their strips of land and instead being allocated to farmers and landowners for whom they had to work, receiving wages rather than producing their own food. The National School is on the left and the only other surviving building (1995) is at the far end of the road.

Charlton House Wantage

Charlton House, c. 1907. Charlton House was situated behind the present Wantage Hospital with grounds extending to forty three acres. William Price was the first owner and the Revd Henry Rudge Hayward built the lodge in Charlton Road. Mr Henry Denis de Vitre bought the house and estate in 1873, but it fell vacant after his death. German prisoners were kept there during the First World War but the house was later destroyed in a fire. Parts of the estate were sold, eg Garston Lane, and the remainder was bought by the Ministry of Supply in 1947 to build houses for Harwell employees.

Charlton Church, c. 1907. Within months of his arrival in Wantage the Revd William Butler feared that 'dissenters' would build a meeting house in Charlton and the village would be lost to the Church of England. He obtained a suitable site, the old village green, and a simple brick Chapel of Ease was built in 1848 at a cost of £200. The architect was William Butterfield.

Home Farm, Charlton, c. 1930. John Stone bought the Manor of Franklyns in 1778, including the old farm buildings. The farmhouse was originally known as Stone's Farm and became the home of their descendants, the Castles, for three generations. The front of the farmhouse underwent Victorian restoration in 1878 but the back retains its Georgian features. The stables on the left, with hay loft above, also provided accommodation for stable lads. The carthouse had a granary and hay loft. The gate on the left was the entrance to Whitehorne's Farm and the shed on wheels was a chicken house!

Threshing, c. 1890. An interesting old photograph from the 'Castle Archives'. The larger farms usually owned their own threshing machines, but hired the engine which was hauled to the site by horses. The tall chimney was designed to keep sparks away from the straw. Compare the number of people (about twenty) required for this procedure alone, removing the grain from the straw, with modern combine harvesting requiring one man to harvest and thresh simultaneously. Note the staddle stones on the extreme left used to keep the stack off the ground and dry.

Mr and Mrs Enoch Wakefield, c. 1910. Mr Wakefield was a shepherd for most of his life. He worked for Mr A S Castle for thirty years. Mrs Wakefield was formerly Miss Rebecca White of Charlton, the couple had four sons and five daughters. Their cottage looks idyllic, but water was drawn from a well and there was no sanitation, only a privy in the garden, tucked prettily behind the hollyhocks.

Drilling, c. 1920. Mr Jack Ilsley, seen here, and his two sons, Stan and Jim, worked for the Castle family. These two beautiful working horses are pulling a drill with muddy wheels so have probably just finished drilling a crop of mangels, swedes or turnips. The empty seed sacks are piled neatly ready for return. Sacks could be hired by farmers and were avalable from the Sack Hiring buildings in Mill Street.

Loading a hay cart, c. 1905. An early photograph of hay making on Home Farm. A happy activity in good weather, a disastrous time during a wet spell.

Building a hay stack, c. 1910. The early labour intensive method of gathering hay and making a stack was eventually aided by horse power. The horse walked in a circle to power a moving chain with spikes which transported the hay from the waggon and up the elevator. Agricultural labourers were required to load the elevator and build the stack.

Building a hay stack, c. 1920. The horse has here been superseded by motor power. Horses were still required to haul the waggons but this motor-powered elevator heralds the end of the era of importance for the shire horses.

International Tractor 10/20 and Massey Harris Binder, c. 1930. This new 'work horse' is harvesting at Ham Field. Many Wantage people have toiled on this field in the past. The West Hill houses in the background were built after the First World War and the Ham Field houses on this site in the 1930s. The land was bought by the UDC from the Castle family and this marked the beginning of the end for the farms and fields that were once close to the old market town.

Maria Castle, c. 1905. Maria Cartwright from Letcombe Bassett married Albert Stone Castle of Home Farm in 1901. The groom was John Morris, a devoted employee of the family. Maria and her governess cart were a familiar sight around the town.

Farman III Military Biplane, 14 June 1911. Captains C J Burke (pilot) and S D Massy (map reader/observer) of the Royal Flying Corps flew this Farman, carrying the very first British military aircraft serial 'AIR BATTN F 1' on its rudders, from Larkhill (Hampshire) to Port Meadow (Oxford). They left Larkhill at 4.15 am landing at Lattin Down and in the afternoon in a meadow belonging to Mr A S Castle at Charlton and 'were visited by hundreds of people'.

Chestnuts Farm, Charlton, c. 1968. This historic old farmhouse and its adjacent land belonged to the Tomkins family for generations and was rented by the Barnards and Castles of Charlton. The South Wing of the building dated from c. 1580. The Berkshire County Council bought the farm in the 1930s. When Mr Aubrey Pocock gave up the tenancy the house was allowed to deteriorate and was eventually demolished in 1971.

Charlton House Estate, 1963, looking towards Hampden Road across the Humber Ditch. This attractive housing development built from 1947-1950 was designed to preserve the natural contours of the land and with green open spaces. The houses were built to attract employees to the Atomic Energy Research Establishment at Harwell. The existence of Charlton as a purely agricultural village was coming to an end. Further housing developments were to follow.

Eleven
A Glimpse of the Villages

Lockinge, c. 1915. A village replanned by Lord and Lady Wantage with houses dating mainly from 1860. The model cottages have steeply pitched roofs and front gardens sloping down to the village street.

Ardington, c. 1914. Lord Wantage VC, died in 1901 and was buried in Ardington churchyard. The seat was presented by the parishioners in 1902 who remembered him gratefully as a friend and benefactor.

East Challow, c. 1930. East Challow sits on each side of the Wantage to Faringdon road. The building on the hill was Nalder & Nalder's engineering works positioned beside the Wilts & Berks Canal in the previous century.

Grove, c. 1910. Kelly's Directory of 1891 refers to Grove as 'an ecclesiastical parish formed in 1835 out of the parish of Wantage.' Two miles from Wantage, the population in 1881 was 557. Housing development here since the 1950s has raised the population to around 8,000 people.

Letcombe Regis, c. 1928. Thatched cottages line the street, some with timber framing. A Alder lives in the first cottage, where a sarsen stone protects the fence. The cottage was tiled before 1932 and the trees cut down and back.

The celebrated Water Cress Beds, Letcombe Bassett, Wantage.

Letcombe Bassett, c. 1910. On the spring line of the Berkshire Downs and the source of the Letcombe Brook, Letcombe Bassett became known for watercress production. The village was aptly named Cresscombe in Hardy's Jude the Obscure.

East Hanney, the Post Office and Telegraph Office, c. 1919. The Hanney's were called Hean's Island in Eleanor Hayden's Islands of the Vale. A village name with the letters 'ey' on the end indicates an island settlement surrounded by marshland.

West Hanney, c. 1910, depicting the agricultural origins of this village. Here are examples of brick and tiled and stone and thatched cottages. The thatched cottage has since been tiled.

East Hendred, c. 1920. The village's picturesque old houses with half-timbering, brick and plastered elevations and thatched or tiled roofs became the subject of a conservation order in 1970. The village is four miles from Wantage.

West Hendred, c. 1920. The only postcard found to date of West Hendred. The Hare Inn, was so named from the hares that are to be seen in the fields nearby. Eleanor Hayden lived in West Hendred and in her Travels Round Our Village, deplored the number of timber-framed cottages which were disappearing.

Stanford in the Vale, c. 1914. The name Stanford is derived from a 'stoney ford', in this case, over the Ock. The houses were built from mixed materials and around village greens. Limestone came from Faringdon and bricks from local brickworks.

Goosey, School and Green, 1908. Scattered brick and stone houses and a wide expanse of green form this village. The name 'Goosey' refers to the flocks of geese reared on the green in pre-Reformation times.

Denchworth, c. 1910, in a flat area of the Vale. The Fox Inn on the right is easily recognisable. The stone village school was designed by G E Street and the brick houses were built in the 1860s.

Childrey, 1922. A village pond and green provide the focal point for the houses built around them. The Fettiplace family founded a school and almshouses here. The Victorian Reading Room was built in 1904.

Kingston Lisle, c. 1904. A peaceful rural village with brick and chalk thatched cottages typical of those to be found in the Vale of the White Horse.

Sparsholt, Watery Lane, c. 1948. A charming village, 3 miles from Wantage, its cottages and houses, thatched and tiled.

Acknowledgements

The diversity of photographs presented has been made possible by the generosity of the following:

The Trustees and Management Committee of the Vale & Downland Museum Centre, Wantage, who have allowed access to photographs given by local people and held by them. Their support for this book is appreciated.

David and Joanna Castle, of Home Farm Charlton, whose family archives have revealed valuable aspects of life in Wantage and Charlton and who have provided interesting old photographs.

Particular thanks are due to Mrs Akers, John Arbery, Howard and Jeanne Badger, Don Bean, Les Bellinger, Sylvia Burton, Beryl Charles, Gordon Collier, Harry Crooks, Aubrey and Enid Denley, Mrs Fern, Edward Fleetwood, Cynthia Froude, Dennis and Gwen Glaysher, Trevor Hancock, Sue Harrison, Mrs K Henry, Sid Mayo, Peter and Gwen Mulford, Basil Prior, Ted Reeves, Jim Richings, Glyn Roberts, Alan Rosevear.

Also the Wantage Local History Group, whose members and meetings contribute freely and importantly to the history of Wantage. (Committee Lynda Allen, George Cassell, Bill Fuller, Betty Golding, Diana Hughes and Jane Waite).

People of Wantage have shown a great interest in the compilation of these photographs and apologies are given for any names inadvertently omitted.

Information has been obtained from early newspapers and trade directories at the Centre for Oxfordshire Studies and Reading, Swindon and Wantage Libraries. Also documents at the Oxfordshire Archives and Berkshire Record Office.

Books and publications consulted:

The Wantage Tramway, S H Pearce Higgins
The Wantage Tramway, Nicholas de Courtais
The Wilts & Berks Canal, L J Dalby.
Publications on Tramway and Canal by Reg Wilkinson.
A Special Street, Kathleen Philip.
The White Horse Country, Nigel Hammond
Berkshire Village Book, Berks WI